Marine Iguanas
Tails of the Galapagos Islands Series

Young Readers Edition

Written By:

Eric Kiefer

Marine Iguanas

Tails of the Galapagos Islands Series

Copyright © 2014 by DLK Publishing House

ISBN: 978-1-941418-01-7

This book is licensed for your personal enjoyment only.

All rights reserved. In accordance with the U.S. Copyright Act of 1976, the scanning, uploading and electronic sharing of any part of this book without permission of the publisher constitutes unlawful piracy and theft of the author's intellectual property. If you would like to use any material from this book (other than review purposes), prior written permission must be obtained by contacting the publisher. Thank you for your support of the author's rights.

Book Cover Design by Donna Hunter

Cover Photo by Sunsinger (depositphotos)

Welcome to the world of the *Marine Iguana*. It is one of only *seven types of reptiles* that live on the Galapagos Islands off the coast of South America. Let's get to know this distant relative of the mighty dinosaurs.

The Seven Types of Reptiles that live on the Galapagos Islands are the Tortise, Turtle, Iguana, Lava Lizard, Gecko, Snake, and Sea Snake.

5

You might ask, "How does a lizard get on an island hundreds of miles off the coast of South America?" Most scientists believe they floated on trees or *debris* (junk) that may have been swept out to sea by strong storms. In fact, that is how scientists believe many of the life forms on the Galapagos Islands got there.

There are several different islands in the Galapagos and each island has its own special type of marine iguana. Some are bigger, some smaller and some have different colors. They are all related to each other. Sort of like cousins.

We all know you should never judge someone by their looks. Marine iguanas are mean looking with wide eyes and a row of spiky scales that

run down their backs. But, they are fairly gentle **herbivores**, which means they eat nothing but algae, plants and seaweed from the ocean rocks.

Marine iguanas have short, flat faces with hard lizard lips that cover up a set of pretty special sharp teeth. They use these teeth to scrape their dinner off of the rocks out below the ocean surface. They also use their sharp strong claws on all four legs to hold onto the rocks while they eat.

13

Marine iguanas started looking for food in the oceans because the islands did not offer much to eat on land. There were other animals, like the giant tortoise and the land iguana, who all wanted the food, too. So, being peaceful little lizards, the marine iguanas decided to eat at the saltwater buffet!

They get to the underwater rocks by swimming. The marine iguanas have *evolved*, or changed, over millions and millions of years to have long flat tails. They use their tails like a boat oar to push themselves through the strong ocean currents like little lizard torpedoes!

Marine iguanas are kind of clumsy when they are on dry land. With a big flat tail and long sharp

aws, you can imagine they do not run ry well. But, they are very graceful when ey get into the water.

Marine iguanas still need to breathe air even though they spend so much time in the ocean. They can hold their breath for a long, long time. This lets them stay underwater to look for food.

The thing about ocean water is that it can be pretty cold. Marine iguanas are *ectothermic*, often called cold blooded. This means they do not make their own body heat the way that people and other *mammals* do.

A mammal *is an animal that breathes air, has a backbone, and grows hair at some point during its life. In addition, all female mammals have glands that can produce milk.*

Since they do not make their own heat, they need to get heat from somewhere else. And, the warmest thing around is the sun! Like nearly all reptiles, marine iguanas spend a lot of time *basking*, or laying around, in the sun to get warm.

Marine iguanas are normally very dark in color and the dark scales of their skin help them to absorb heat from the sun. When they are good and warm, they can dive into the ocean and search for food. After a while, they start to cool down and therefore need to hit the beach to soak-up some rays!

Since their diet is made up of plants from the ocean, the marine iguanas end up eating a LOT of salt. To keep from getting sick from too much salt, they

have a special gland in their head that helps filter the salt from their blood. When the gland gets full, the iguana blows it out almost like blowing your nose when you have a cold.

All those salty boogers end up drying out on the marine iguana's head. It can make them look like they are wearing George Washington's wig! As gross as it sounds, it shows that the marine iguanas are eating well and that they are in good health.

Now, do not run off and tell your parents or your teachers that you want to be like a healthy marine iguana with salt boogers all over your head. It is healthy for iguanas, but it is still kind of gross for people!

Healthy adult marine iguanas do get together during their mating season. Mating season is about the only time that our peaceful little friends can turn a little nasty. The males can be very aggressive to each other when they are trying to find females to mate with.

Male and female marine iguanas look pretty much alike except that the males can be a little bigger than the

females. During mating season, the males' skin can become a little more colorful. The extra color helps them look good for the ladies!

Once mating season is over, the female marine iguanas have to dig holes in the ground where they can lay their eggs. She has to dig the hole just right so it stays warm enough for the eggs to develop, but not so hot that they become fried eggs! If all goes well, in about four months, the eggs hatch and baby iguanas emerge from the hole.

Back when marine iguanas first made their home on the Galapagos Islands, they did not have any *predators*, or animals that would hunt them for food. But, since man found the islands, their boats accidentally introduced foreign animals like rats, cats and dogs to the island. This has been bad news for the marine iguanas there.

Adult marine iguanas can take care of themselves against even the hungriest cats or dogs. But iguana eggs and baby iguanas make tempting meals for all those new predators. Mother iguanas will guard their nests for a while, but the babies are on their own from the moment they hatch.

The marine iguanas are learning to live with these new threats just like they learned to live on their island home millions of years ago. What they cannot adapt to, though, are changes to their environment like oil spills and pollution. We humans need to do everything we can to help save the environment so animals like the marine iguana can survive for many more millions of years.

Marine iguanas are now considered to be a Vulnerable threatened species. This means that if we don't actively find ways to protect

them from pollution and invasive predators, they might not survive without our help. Let's all do what we can to help save them!

If you want to learn more about marine iguanas, check with your local zoo or aquarium. Many of them have marine iguanas and you could see them up close without having to go all the way to the Galapagos Islands! You can also find out more about marine iguanas by looking on the internet.

Remember to always get permission from your parents or your teacher before going online. You can check out:

www.nationalgeographic.com

as well as many fine works by the famous naturalist **Sir David Attenborough**. We sure hope you want to learn as much as you can about marine iguanas and all the wonderful living things that make up our incredible planet!

Author note: I want to send out a HUGE thank you to all those who took such amazing photos and are willing to share. This book could NOT exist without your amazing work. Thank you, again.

Eric Kiefer

PHOTOGRAPHS © 2014: pg 1 (Depositphotos - shalamov), pg 5 (Depositphotos - SURZet), pg 6 (Flickr - Ben eBaker), pg 8 (Depositphotos - SURZet), pg 10-11 (Flickr - blinking idiot), pg 12 (Depositphotos - pxhidalgo), pg 13 (Depositphotos - Wirepec) pg 14 (Flickr - Alan), pg 16 (Adriana Vidal), pg 17 (Flickr - Derek Keats), pg 18 (Flickr - Rein Ketelaars), pg 19 (Flickr - Antje Schultner), pg 21 (Depositphoto - sergeydolya), pg 23 (Flickr - Alan Harris), pg 24 (Depositphoto - paulvandenberg), pg 25 (commons. wikimedia.org - D. Gordon E. Robertson), pg 26 (Flickr - Mark Putney), pg 27 (Flickr - NH53), pg 28-29 (Depositphotos - eskymaks) pg 30 (Depositphotos - kjorgen), pg 31 (Flickr - mountainamoeba), pg 32 (Depositphotos - sunsinger), pg 34 (Flickr - Rick Bergstrom), pg 35 (Flickr - Andrew Turner), pg 36-37 (Flickr - Linda Paul), pg 39 (Shutterstock - Matt Tilghman), pg 40 (Flickr - Linda Paul), pg 42 (Yves Vallier), pg 45 (Flickr - Antje Schultner), pg 46-47 (Depositphotos - kjorgen), pg 49 (Flickr - John Solaro), pg 50 (Flickr - Charles Sharp)

All images provided by Flickr or government agencies are under Creative Commons License. All others have been purchased via Royalty Free websites.

53

www.ingramcontent.com/pod-product-compliance
Lightning Source LLC
Chambersburg PA
CBHW041928040426
42444CB00018B/3467